THE TINIEST MUZZLE
SINGS SONGS OF FREEDOM

MAGDALENA ZURAWSKI

WAVE BOOKS

THE TINIEST MUZZLE
SINGS SONGS OF FREEDOM

SEATTLE & NEW YORK

Published by Wave Books            www.wavepoetry.com

Copyright © 2019 by Magdalena Zurawski            All rights reserved

Wave Books titles are distributed to the trade by Consortium Book Sales and Distribution

Phone: 800-283-3572            SAN 631-760X

Library of Congress Cataloging-in-Publication Data

Names: Zurawski, Magdalena, author.

Title: The tiniest muzzle sings songs of freedom / Magdalena Zurawski.

Description: First edition. | Seattle : Wave Books, 2019.

Identifiers: LCCN 2018033740 | ISBN 9781940696836 (limited edition hardcover) | ISBN 9781940696843 (trade pbk.)

Classification: LCC PS3576.U543 A6 2019 | DDC 811/.54—dc23

LC record available at https://lccn.loc.gov/2018033740

Designed and composed by Quemadura            Printed in the United States of America

9 8 7 6 5 4 3 2 1            First Edition

Wave Books 077

est M

gs of

## OF LIBERATION

You arrive in a sentence
where you would like
to stay, but you are told

to move on to another,
so you do and wish only
this time to keep to imaginary

places. You are not
given Zanzibar or Timbuktu
but Paducah where two

soldiers compare figures on
a motel balcony. You
note the exits and a sign

announcing no free breakfast.
One says, "You look good, man,"
to the other, who nods. Though

you had always understood
figures differently, you
respect their loyalty

2

to a cause impossible
to understand. "I've been
through two surgeries and

still smell as fresh as
a piano," the admired one
says. The moon is quartered,

and the air is mild. You
sleep in a rented bed
overlooking asphalt. Through

the vents your German
professor repeats, "Ich komme
aus Dodge. Woher kommst Du?"

over and over until your
True Being separates
from a cough that will not

go away. The professor in
the morning seeks out your eye
as he slips out the door,

"To be in a sentence,"
he asserts, "is by
nature to be passing through."

## ISLAND PILL

You are surely lost.     The waiting room
                                      is teeming
                         with pigeons.

Your birthday cake
takes off
and   eats
     some horse.

Here, take this pill.
          It knows Vladimir. It knows
                         communists of all nations. It says
kids everywhere love life. And intend
to love life     beyond music        beyond breath.

If the Russian comes by
at midnight in the rain, just say, hey, Vlad.
Poets *are* assholes, tender
lambs of electricity. They have
mouths of mind open to the tone-deaf wind and
a sweet smack of "Ah, thanx, I needed that."

(Their hearts shine pure with the moon
and swim to Satin Island true as midnight sky pollution.)

Oh, to have birds cooing,
bells ringing, tofu frying, and unusually
high energy levels!

To feel that stealthy familiar of a new poem coming up mechanical on the clank machine!

It carries you through a wall.
It knows just what you mean.

## THIS ONE HYDRA

FOR FRED MOTEN AND LAURA HARRIS

What was I doing
      turning cheeks
beneath a sagging roof
        myself askew in cheap carpet?

For relief I
took a seat
on a cloud.

There I spoke
it to dust.
      It did
me good.

When I finally
looked at my
own two hands

I had to name
one Weary and
the other Skull.

Together we cut
the landlady's cord
which had denied us

money even in our
sleep. I let a
small crowd

of anglers and
prigs below know
how she bludgeoned

me, how an officer
said it was just
an owl who had

plucked my head.
It made my heart
heavy enough

for a hand truck.
I urged the men
to wander the

streets with
gasoline, the women
to strike matches.

As for the future
I will refrain
from the indoors

from living upon
floorboards and
stairs where long

before I was born
I was meant to expire.

## SANTA MONICA

She didn't say anything
I hadn't heard. I had a gram
of her in my mouth.

The dawn is emotions, so she and I went
purely physical, spinning on one toe
in damp sand, the stars slipping yellow & knifing
out a place in us.

It was
our place &
there we slept,
Earth.

She said the thoughts
on my face saw me
and that I winced too often.
Her advice gave me
    the mountains and a flight path.

(It's a dirty dawn
  the pink spark
    of Santa Monica,

a light of sweet yawns, slow,

a dog cloud

another life to know.)

MY LIFE IN POLITICS

Incapable of limiting themselves to petty
offenses, my hands broke into my chest and choked
every slumbering deity.
                    After that I no longer cared
to argue about the nature of the flesh. Whether powered by vitalist or
mechanical forces, the spirits had in either case evaporated
as easily as life from the nostrils of a drowned man.


                    Oddly, I did begin to care about numbers, but only in exchangeable forms.
"Bread," I heard a man say once
        and it made me a depressive materialist, not
unlike a Franciscan without a dove. I collected frozen peas, greeting each one
like a lost friend, then dispersing them in green streams to the hungry mouths
in the surrounding counties.


                    At home I have an old painting to comfort me, a fine example
of Impressionism from the Eastern bloc circa 1981. In the subtle oranges
singeing the trees one sees the foreshadowing of martial law.


                    As a child I sat in my Western living room and watched
            the Molotov cocktails fly behind the Iron Drape. Back then no one thought
to explain to me how walls against the flight of capital might end in flames,
how on TV I was witnessing soldiers clip the wings of the very same paper birds
                            that here flew all around me.

## THAT MUST BE A DUCK

The Indian food was mediocre
but I thought it only
right that we too should
feel the effects of war.

I had been very influenced
by Russia and often fell
asleep thinking of Ivan and
his brothers, of smoked eel,

and of oligarchs. "Come," I told
my mother. "I know where
the coffee is still good."
Our bicycles were hidden

behind a snowbank guarded
by peasants. My mother gave
them a ten-dollar bill, then said,
"When the machine breaks,

we break." They held it
to the light. At the edge
of the city in the clearest
of water we found the dogs

that had adapted. They swam
deep using their wings
as fins. One broke through
the surface. "Look, Ma, they've

mastered land, sea, air." "No,
that's not possible. That must
be a duck," she insisted.
"But, Ma," I said pointing,

"look, his face. A terrier."

MOPE

This room has
only the rhythm of

flesh turned on
too soon. Someone's
laughter sunsets behind

false air and
I come up
drenched in red
dots and iron

floes. Deep in
my nervous system
a sky fills

with frosted chatter.
I'm done. Finally
down. It's clear:

I've earned nothing.

## SOMEPLACE IN YOUR MOUTH

When the line of heads continued
through the city in a sliver
of tattered oxygen, you were a sensation

to plunge into—a way of busting life
out of swollen eyes or fingering
a piano in sleep. The streets

were banknotes—rich densities of
flesh adjacent to freedom. You
pissed in them and devoured the light

floating from the book's skin. Cash
was the only thing bringing life
to the pavement, so you and I vanished

with resolve and fucked in space un-
occupied. Dusk created its shimmer and
melted us with mercy into the outer realms.

## LENTEN TELETHON

Falling through

feelings only to

aspire to sleep

Let the comma come

take your head

                & tilt the dream open

(Can't you isolate

a tone to           slash some anguish?

Won't you wind off       an old ear?

Could you       let yourself       some glee?)

## LADIES LOVE ADJUNCTS

FOR JENNY GROPP

She told me
to take
a large plate

for my troubles   then
as we roamed
the house I tried

not to draw his eye
to the fact that
we had fucked

but I was tempted
to make her want
me so I stood

still     a tree amid
wood   did it work

yes

it let me assert
myself while he talked
about Hong Kong

in the other
room   though I knew
she hadn't minded

the other night   then he
and the student got
distracted by

two bums fighting
near his car

            I took the chance
    and grabbed her elbow
              opened

the cellar door   Quick
I said   I'll follow
you to the furnace

## FOR THE REPUBLIC

The way I'm strapped into myself
I can't escape. Wake up and be a better person! Clip your toenails,
and by sunrise make sure

        you're sitting at the table reading Arendt.

With a little focus
I could become
everything I ever wished
to be: levelheaded and
buoyed,

    a real (wo)man of conviction. But no, at night,

        I'm like an old towel on the line, tossing and

        turning in the wind of the dear leader's

        words. What does

      it matter if I grind

    my teeth for the old ladies of

    Puerto Rico? Or take a knee

    in the front yard every time I hear

    the national anthem

    in my head? The neighbor just thinks

    I'm weeding and waves.

BOTH RAPID AND NOT RAPID


Where had the state placed your crutches?
By now you are on your own,      a salesclerk roaming the parking lot.


Clouds arrive faster than furniture. You look up and tell yourself,
"Even the low trees are catching wind."


Only a man who
no longer knows              what life means
                            contents himself
                                    with describing how it looks.


            You know this, of course.
                    If only you could stuff your own bugle, you might hide the betrayal.


        To be fair nobody said the business would suit you. Even your mother
        (despite the new tires) had her doubts. The lead apron you are forced
        to wear does weigh a soul down. And the dust in the newspaper (there's
        always dust in the newspaper) only bores and empties
        your face, stops you
        from putting thought
                    to paper.

Last night before bed you read Blake and for a minute you were (like him)
convinced that your mind was the form of God. You knew
something could beautifully erupt inside you and interrupt this doubt.

As the moon shone in your window, you believed it all deeply. You would do
anything to live in such reward.

Now, all of a sudden, a gust of dust whips up to blind you.
In such cloud you think, "Remember, you have earned this chair."
You wait for the delivery to round the corner, and just like that you
acquire a clean-shaven authority. With a stately posture
you overcome the look of your flimsy attire, but nothing undresses
the look in your eyes, the gaze of someone undone, a living half-shut.

## THE WAKE

Dreams change in thoughts bounce
to clarity in the street our sense of living sparks errors
consistent        with life

so
the odd dream
aerial and marshy

gets hammered into the solid lines
of a face—the chance

of another
life now frozen into

old dictate

PARAKEET

She remembers only the pops of the record and his voice scratched full of tongues, how
       it muscles with the silt of each broad grin that had ever
                 nursed it with praise.

     How he owns a universe through the flesh of
     his mouth,
     she says, is cut deep
     into the tissue of her brain, pressed hard into that organ
     by way of the way he says
            the word "change."

She doesn't even know if she's heard it before or
if she had long ago too often heard someone's memory of it and
made it her own. But now she can go deeper into the vinyl, through its
grooves, come out the other side, and wring him with her
own hands, finally make him the parakeet.

## IT'S HARD TO BE A SAINT

I was sympathetic to language, but often
it shrugged me and kept other lovers.
I crawled through the commas of

Romanticism and rejected the rhythms,
though sometimes at night I could feel
a little sad. I could emerge now

into a new kind of style, but the market
is already flooded and my people
have lost faith in things meant to land

a clear yes or no. It's good to welcome
a stranger into the house. Introduce her
to everyone sitting at the table and wash

your hands before you serve her, lest
the residue of other meals affect your
affections. "If something is beautiful we do

not even experience pain as pain." (A man said
that.) "I think I owe all words to my friends."
(I said that.) "We speak to one another

in circles alone with ourselves." (He said
that, too.) That's why we go to war.
We've gotten too big to be friends with

everyone and so I like to feel the fellowship
of the person next to me shooting
out across a foreign plain. The streams

of light on the horizon are something
I share with him and this is also a feeling
of love. I spoke to his widow and touched

his dog. I told his daughter how his last breath
was Homeric and spoke of nothing but returning home.

## THE PROBLEM

The problem—there was no longer a natural way to write. My hand,

     the musculature of my hand, could no longer speed the pen to my thoughts.

I had worked too long on the machines.

The computer was just a television

and so seemed

     only a way to distract me

     from my writing

     rather than preserve it.

The typewriter could give me speed, but paper seemed so easy to burn.

Should the house go up in flames, how would I edit the next draft?

          Also, one had

            to be both exactly right on the first try and capable of later

          locating each page in the house.

And how could

so much paper

not feel like scraps,

drafts, sorry attempts

unzapped into virtual

existence?

Instead, I wrote in thought at the edge of sleep,

so that my best poems disappeared just as I began to dream. I know I was their only audience, but I am sure they were my best work. If only I knew how to retrieve them, knew where they were stored.

## NIGHT CLASS

What did it mean "to put a matter
to rest," the metaphor eluded her.

"No one, nothing needed sleep," I persisted.
"We simply no longer have a need to talk

about it, whatever it may be." I had the
language and an ability to create examples.

I, like all pedagogues, could keep
beauty before me in a chair, and

I didn't put the matter to rest but
persisted in explaining, "No one, nothing

was asleep. We simply had no need to talk
about it anymore." That face. She had that

face only found in movies and in dreams,
those places where I still moved with desire.

Still, I was removed from the classroom, reunited
with my trusted companion, though I hadn't known

that he, like my trusted notebook, had also gone missing after I had taken the escalator.

Now he was having a martini at the bar despite dogs being banned from the establishment.

THE LIP


The lip
is a memory
of feel

and how
soft it
is with

its want-
ing of
a green

life some-
one had
once brack-

eted for
me—
a paren(t)-

thesis I
could not
enter.

(A mother
sees you
at birth

as no other.)

## MIDWINTER DAY

I was in hollow sleep that angled
from my nerves. The book I found
was a new flower, one I had once

before not seen and tonight it
would not let me rest. I tried
to fall but wanted the poems as

my own. I knew this made me
a kind of spirit not but barely
a soul and was with this also

weighed down in just worry.
How many books I've read that
I was not ready for! I'll spend

a life rereading what I before
thought to know but couldn't.

JULY 2016

When it became clear
that I should produce I

fell into a hole and shat ideas
while outside, bodies

disappeared in political
light. "If we return," you

said, "living will bleach
the thin tissue of our wits."

We huddled wounded,
our vacant ulcers bound

with visions. "Stand up and
be counted," I tried to say—

instead, I looked out
a window and shivered.

A FOLD OF SUN

We decided
I should go
alone on foot.

I would find
him in the
pharmacy. If

he said "In the
head of God
all propositions

have existed
always," we would
make the exchange.

He was standing
in front of the
calamine lotion.

He spoke to
the air. I slipped
the envelope

into his pocket
and bought a topical
analgesic to

avoid suspicion.
When I left, I had
a face again,

could open an
account, drink
coffee in

the sun. On the street
two women talked
of money. I paid

them no mind. I
could now walk
with my light

always to the front.

## THE REMAINDERS

FOR DUNCAN AND BLASER

1

If you studied business
in school you studied rules and
principles you learned
that business is work done

by animals a team of horses
will thresh three hundred bushels
a day and even one horse
with a twenty-five-dollar machine

can be good business a horse
that eats only a moderate quantity
of food will do as much business
as one that eats continually and

men hired to mend harnesses
must be kept busy mending
harnesses if you are to do good
business a supervisor needs no

experience he must only consult
analyze and explain the beauty
of business is that there are
many animals to do it for you

should you not care for horses
several pharmacists will fill
prescriptions all day long and
several doctors will write

prescriptions for every patient
even a pecan farm if supervised
correctly can be good business
as long as Billy drives the shaker

through the orchard once
the shuck has split and Jim
sweeps the fallen nuts into
windrows and the harvesters

follow to load the nuts into
wagons make sure your grade B
nuts are separated out by
quality control "Mammoth Pecans"

can vary a great deal in
size from one season to
the next you will know
you have supervised nut

production well if Jean sends
a note stating your packing
and shipping is exceptional
business is work done by animals

all the world is an animal a good
businessman is a zookeeper
you learned this in school
poetry however is something else


2


I had found the book among the remainders the pages almost empty with words and
when I was quiet they heard me and found the little soul inside me large enough to open
themselves there into an elsewhere where I resided and often invited you too and one
night a single word opened to me to repeat itself as if I were its instrument I was helpless
in its cycle it began not unlike a school lesson simple sentences

*the weather broke*
*the bough broke*
*my voice broke*

that's where it began and it did not stop there my mouth would not tire and it let loose
every *break* it could have known so that at 3 a.m. if you had entered the room you would
have found me muttering

*my heart is breaking and my eyes are dim*

*and above me*
*the billows break*

     *I have the delusion that no*
     *campaign can break*
     *the neck of this rebellion*

          *a bank breaks and on every side of me workmen are discharged*

     *the hounds break the fox*
     *while the gentlemen watch*

*most of their bombs break before they fall and there is no breath of air to break the wave*

and so on I spoke until finally the words released me
into Virgil and had me thrice utter

     *verse breaks the ground*
     *verse breaks the ground*
     *verse breaks the ground*

shortly before dawn     I was desperate for sleep

     when I awoke the world had not changed so I asked myself
where is it that you choose to live and then in the constellation of trees behind the house
I saw a door of light and there I entered and took on the light and felt my elsewhere
breaking loose and I said to the world business is work done by animals but poetry is
something else

3

There's something in a word that remains outside
watches the hounds break up a fox

> The weather brought
> an injured deer
> near the door
> so I would
> know that our
> commonwealth is grief—
> the most unstable
> element of language—
> that vowel unsettled
> in the mouth

it had been raining seven days and seven nights and we had grown used to
sitting in the dark
if they had come with their guns I would have told them
about the strip mall a bookstore of remainders on metal shelves what's the shame of poetry
I would have said but no one came

4

and I said to myself that other,

Soldier, care for the O in the poem
and take on light
become astral

but my flesh, Sir,
remains here, I said, I am
so reasonable it leaves me
a failed escape,

Soldier, I said, there is a door
a break there in the mountain
if you will a there there

no, Sir, I said, all the world
is an animal and I am an animal and
the poem is an animal,

Soldier, I said, I command you to the field
I command you to make the words
an elsewhere

but, Sir, I said, each time I return
to the field I see nothing but animals
I know nothing but animals, Sir,

they have made my mind into nothing but animal,

Soldier, I command you, lift your snout up

RONEO ROOM TRIPTYCH

How do you find it at first, so I lay there normal, waking in sleep maybe a someone in myself. I should have felt need or grown a person I couldn't stand in my throat. I wanted to work myself *into* real people or mostly I didn't. Maybe I still do. I don't always have to feel good. You know what the heart does? It accepts being as texture. Exercises my not being into a song of parallel life. I don't know. Maybe I can't and still do.

\*

I hid this head in a calm blanket against a back wall. Don't see me. As if never wanting this what once was skirting all around and don't worry, I'm all right. Never there is this world I dream but here I'm part museum. Why dress what you lent away? I guess to think some way of being home but my head hurt. How to animal again. Fall off table, scramble into hole. Had once I known skin and liked it, dared in lapping and licking and folded some future into it, anyhow, you fill up the house even though I'm not here. I wake seamstressing in sleep.

\*

I was just waking when the best things started to happen in pictures. Had the words now timed to make a little something of themselves in the margin of speech. It's your stage, the world, but home, it's parenthetical space, it's living. It goes down into its own English. A poet is a frame not beauty in a window. Do you see me waving?

## SUMMER IN THE NETWORK OF PRIVILEGED CARPORTS

FOR DANIEL BOUCHARD

In my body there is a death
I will always
want to forget

    I see it
up ahead in the clearing of
my breath I'm alive
in a yard where I look
for life I find a fawn caught
    between two posts and call
    for help

    I drive the machine
    through ivy
    take down the privet
    don't stall the engine the blades
    don't hesitate but
    the turf grass won't give up
    its turf like a tired
        proverb I sing against the machine
        sound a hole    an O

in which my heart dwells

how I'm wronged and well fed
O to think of the flies
and hummingbirds and wasps

to think how I have tried to kill
the fire ants     how I have tried to harm
no living thing

except the fire ants
how I have ignored the diseased
retirees who keep the weeds
down with Roundup®

how I want the lavender and
the foxgloves and lemon tree to live and

is it here
in all this

grunt and feeling that our lived lives expand?
I take care of the hedges can't
keep up with things in the carport

the problem of existence is rarely
addressed in carports

or maybe I should open the fridge
take out the mayonnaise
make a sandwich and shut up

this is life / with a butter knife

The soil washes
down the hill to
the street there
the sediment of
the gutter becomes
a rich ground for

        everything green
           the armadillos hide
       in the mint and pineapple sage
the basil and
lemon balm are all gnawed
           but not the rosemary
             the rosemary withstands the heat

    the bench
    with the
    broken board
    I fixed
    for my forty-
    third birthday

the grill that leaks grease and the mice
that feast on the grease and the hose
that got nicked

the faucet now capped with
a blue plastic bucket

                                another fawn
rejected by its mother
the fox who stole the neighbor's chicken the copperhead dead
        under Clayton's
                magnolia

I return to the carport with dirt
in my shoe and a rash from grazing
cukes everything I own seems broken
even after it's been fixed
an old Snapper with a severed
fuel line seeds for black-eyed peas
dryer fuzz blown into a gas spot

And then this:

dish soap
salt
and
white
vinegar

ready
to snuff out any leaf
        I'd like not to live

## DOES MY LIP LIMP?

          The birds light
my return with foam
                          but a thousand
          still remain rapid. How was it
          that a bridge
bent forward toward
my walking?


          My memory's a fragile hollow
behind the raven's nest and the eyelashes
                    I forget
                    and break someone returns
                              to me
                    for living.


The ruins
          ladder forth and compose
a seething unity. I'm hungry
                          a swelter of skull   that feels its lack.


                    Is talking shallow torture
for you? I find it flat

when in mind I no longer entertain

toward a new world.


Will it start? Does any thought float?

## SOME COLLIDE

The roof's on golden rain
drifting a city into itself

and space swings silver—wets the trillioned air

drops each
world adrift
into a gutter

the street and the stone split light like it's an apple—the light overloaded and spun

the moon makes gravity a shine path of
       sensation—freedom to all bodies and
              skies and words

NATURAL SKIN

The poem is a pair of eyes
moving a nose
down a page

        and
        soft is the world outside
        —bread and dust

    light
    on our hands turns to mist through
the thought we are through

our
head's the best
meaning
in it

ELL FIRE

I don't traverse

      with demons to hang there

in      dust

      light

but only

for the voices

           loose

      human

That was all it took. One pesky
minute adrift in the mind
at bedtime. Awake there, I didn't sleep, naked and
unconsoled. Why did God always insist
on using brains to store unwanted
soundtracks? I stretched my legs, walked the dog, and still
"truth" wouldn't fall out of my ear. It gave me
a stiff neck and a strange gait. As unhappy
as a bird in snow, I sat down to plan
at the kitchen table with the Formica at my elbows.
My companion felt suddenly the seriousness of
the problem. It was, then, easy to explain. Getting
to go where you aren't, where you never will be, that's
what airplanes are all about, I began. Nescafé,
diesel fumes, Nietzsche's typewriter behind
a pane of glass, how wonderful it will be
to stay where we can never live. She clearly understood. And only
a short walk from the S-Bahn station, I noted, the lovers
are buried, through the woods, interred where they fell, by the lake.
With this last detail she packed her trunks.

We admired the shapes of foreign spoons, the slightly
different cut of shirt worn by men over 50. Had we
the chance, we would have even found an Italian
railroad yard worthy of our attention. And when
an elderly Danish woman at the next table inquired finally
how it was that our countrymen were so stupid, I could only
note that historically our army's firing lines have been circular.

## INNOCENCE ISN'T WHAT APPEARS

I used to ground my need by falling down an etymology
　　　　I stood upon infirm because nothing
in sight was vision or appeared real

　　　　　a thing that felt
hidden rose always before me clouded this world remained then simple illegible

　　　　and maybe *phantasm*
is a room Dante keeps open in the head　　embalmed a word there in stone sensation

a grasped idea to
keep moving in time

　　　　or is there no real

　　　　but at night I think of one night
　　　　in a pool above ground at night as a child I saw lights shed in the silk of water

　　　　and my eyes to the sky and
there enfolded my mind in an open
beyond all church sisters inducing heaven

a child feels easily
eternal boredom in eternity
such terror an empathy for what's empty    it's not easy to let my mind fall there
or once was    I think still very little through idea
only feel a loneliness in an eternal

## MOM'S THE BOON INSIDE OUR SKULLS


To munch Sparkles we cram the Lawn
with Vice
and jump
                        the Street lifts and the Sky
stays up late stoned and talking

Mom
floats the back Porch   hops the Fence and
amputates herself from our best Airwave

back inside lesser Earth
she waves
a Sausage sweetly   opens our Minds
            to Bags of Cheeseburgers

by second Bite
            the warmth of Day jets through
to ruffle the Clothes
we're not wearing            our Bodies palm the restive State

How we slip out
the sweet Heat of the Love
that fleshed us!

THE TINY ACHES


Sometimes things hurt like a dream
in the flesh. You are seeking a huge
pair of butterflies

               who you know will only come later. Four a.m. keeps ringing.
Its spidery snare and all the stars are
your own headache cemented in our most ancient fears. Even love
     emerges as just
a plush yawn, a hydroponic mood of lingering
limbs. It chews the warm light
slowly,
     as if you might
not be here.         Its idiot words refuse to reveal
         their intent.


      You wake muffled.
Is there any tenderness on deck?


      The present is not enough, will never be
enough. The future,
artificial and polite, promises you a locomotive
heading west. You feel it coming
through the patio beneath your feet.

You will arrive, someone tells you. There will be a treelined belonging. You will finally
shed the tiny aches of your birth. Someone else sees

the doubt in your face and assures you
every little flower is the craft of
someone you haven't yet met. You nod, lift a leg as if preparing to board,
though you don't hardly believe it.

COOL ARK FOR CLARK

These pleasures of the breath-husk
are merely for frolic's sake. Have
them on toast! Earth is doing

backflips on a leash. Your car
heaves, but I listen only
to your heart. Yes—the mind

shakes the treetops and the water
glass. You can hurl comets if you
open the senses but stay casual.

Keep the green window plants,
pickled newspapers, and a table
for two near the waxed

genitals. We have enrolled in a good
college, so take no guff. Let your spirits

blow your nose into the brain where
a world revolves around a fine bacterium.

I'VE ALWAYS GOT SOMEONE

In the yard I was dreaming
in a firefly with the tomatoes
and heard some words rest too easy
against my cheek. The coneflowers were
bending their feet.
       I thought,

in this wind
whoever's dead will call me.

I was
a little levitated and relaxed.
This allowed everything
coming through the trees
       to sweep into me. When I opened my eyes it was noon
and the dog was sharpening
his cuspid just like that ghost

I could never find. Pete rang
and said, wave if you're in trouble.

## A SALVE IS LESS THAN SALVATION

Life is always the same fragility appearing in a different bloom, so naturally
    you should go outdoors to collapse.

        Forget that the possibility of quiet rescue is bound
        by a dark wood absent of any Beatrice.    Think instead,
                the summer's almost at winter.
            The balmy birth of Christ awaits us, even if once it
            melts away, nothing but water will remain.

I make no promises, but if you're ready, my name is George.
Like all spirits I'm now under corporate contract and
in uniform, but ignore the red tape. Focus on my forehead. Unload everything
    into the worry lines of eternity. And here,
    at my mouth, though the color passes for sand, there's
    a basin in which to unload the past, a space I've masked
    as a haul of disintegrating twigs porous to the touch.

Remember, the light of tepid dreams is almost worthless. When the words of the world are
only half-strange, remain seated and pretend to tie your shoe. Entangle your letters in per-
cepts as fragrant as wisteria overtaking dim fields. No longer be satisfied with mild comforts,
those shelters that hinder real blossoming.

## AS SOLID

Joe
moans low
under clouds
in a town with only one payroll.
                    Did you know
                    Columbus
knew this town
was round?

Joe knows it's flat.
        It's filled
with potholes and
two sons of no
ones. It's scrubbed. Everyone is loose-
livered.

Joe knows there's no place to go,
so he digs in. Forgets up. He holds

steady, keeps his soul resident, solid,
as solid as
closed space is open.

LIFE FOR MIKE

Shit flows downstream
on big pills and
your pal's a loony
on timed-release spirit.

He's the width
of a wolf all animated
in gray along
a highway. Traffic's
a mode of worry
so worry.

Your breath hits
the outskirts of Pensacola while
California bangs in
your shirt. Your
heaven is windy and
there's no more wine.

Call for help.
Where is there a sign
willing to understand?

DARK WILLIAM

dark William,

hop out of bed, skirt this oncoming breeze,

and repopulate the CAUSE!

                           Life is giving you

new glands, crossed-wire circuitry, and all the Jesus

in Maui. No doubt, the bay's an ample mouth, a thread, a string.


Lights shoot through stars, so when next you dream

see that clearing in the cutaway sky.


Still, I know, these spirits are heavy in the dark—the same

        dark you lie in now

          a charge pulsing through the brain

where Life sits

in its dirty shirts.

                    But there *is* a Brooklyn Bridge, a ginger ale,

and a check in the mail: you're breathing, dark William.

Just fly open over the world, fear-bound by nothing.


Leave this false Eternity as easy as morning!


Sure, history is carbon-charred air. Smoke it.

You are molten nectar, an iris full of glare, a brightness

in all of this, that too-much that binds us.

So think this dark finally
so final, dark Will. Laugh it all up and push
through some final whimper. Be as boy-man as you can and FLY
out this heat-hammered cloud of night.

## LOPSIDED AGAINST MY HEART

My head's an ol' bag of rice floating on a stem. Something
the poem wants to pull onto the shores of Lake Bliss. Go ahead,
make me sway! Water is liquid, but love can only ride a wave

until its wide smile makes a boo-boo. It's boring. Trust me, I *am*
alive even if I'm sick of crickets at night and poking into that hot
stick you point into the breeze. My blanket's always crying, but it

blows its own nose across dreams wherein desire congeals and
skunks my pain in a junked car drunk and drinking. The summer's dry
afternoon limps oceanward and heaves as I read to dead trees without

teeth or heroes. Please, I ask, serve love lightly. Do not flood my face
with feeling. I'm trying not to arouse hot tears. I'm on the rocks with gin and
hurt by winds and when I finally fall into speech, "We are alone," I say.

It comes half-baked. At least this thin flower maintains
it knows me so my fancies and fears remain a kind beauty.

TO A BANKER

Suckled in a market suit you emit a rot fog and with
your shovel up     gimp to
any John Pop and omit him 'til he obits empty

POEM

I turned my back to the light and instead considered the pigeons
while the landlords ate the delicate
                    flesh of young artichokes

                and cut a door off from its frame
and scraped the sleep off a body that wanted most to be alone.

            "He jumped from a tree and broke his leg!" the story goes.

The empty music
of a bus
slid someplace else and skimmed
across the sweat
of fingers striking flint.

Later I calmed my head
and split the bud of a green rose
as if to bloom an action in my arms.

I visited small dots on the skyline from a window while drinking
cold coffee and scratched a flea from everything
I could describe. Nothing could put me back together again. The red bird with
the orange beak or the yellow moth with the blue stripe.

I marched in a circle.

I bathed in a tub.

I heard shots fired across the radio.

I got agitated with the announcer.

An attic fan circulated the water that hung in the air.

The tedium came at me in slight angles.

Now I am here.

Shall I dry myself in the lapping sea or put the smoke of oceans on the rocks of your eyes?

# HIGH MIST TOWARD NOON

Instituted at the desk but not yet overcome
by the banality at the end of imagination, you ask
the page: will all tongues
run dry? You're invested personally.

A light so trumpetlike in its tone knuckles the breeze,
    but it's a blue world no matter how brassed. Whole books
    are left undigested, while the telephone maintains its place
    as the object of every preposition.

The down on an arm can, however, on occasion, stand on end,
as if your skin sensed an open field behind the bursting silence.
There the wild globe perspires in its desire to overcome the limits
of your landscape, like something endangered and alive slinking
away from the tiled agenda of a roadside restroom. Your eye
now unimpressed by donuts and funnel cakes finds a stellar
sequence of moons rising through the pines above a morning.

When back in your office you see a kid grate his teeth against
a sentence hollowing through the static of the intercom, you inform
the clerk in a short-sleeve shirt that the time has come:
you must rearrange your life. You command him to cuff you and

in a set of disposable restraints, you become a saint, arrested and
arresting. Your eyes full of suffering turn to the ceiling tiles, through
which your gaze pierces to a beyond of copper wires
in vinyl casings—yellow, green, and blue—linking you to every terrestrial
being above and below your floor,

     an elevator of voices,

          an orphic infinity.

uzzl

of Fre

## ACKNOWLEDGMENTS

Thank you to the editors of the following journals for publishing some of the poems in this collection: *Bennington Review*, *Berkeley Poetry Review*, *Cordite Poetry Review*, *La Vague Journal*, *New American Writing*, *Oversound*, *Poem-a-Day* from the Academy of American Poets, *The Recluse*, *Sonora Review*, and *Spoon River Poetry Review*.

Thanks to Michelle Koerner and Joseph Massey for reading early versions of this collection.

My deepest gratitude to Joshua Beckman for listening to my work so carefully and to Heidi, Ryo, Blyss, and everyone else at Wave for helping to bring this book into the world.

Love and thanks to Gina Abelkop for always believing in what I'm doing and for helping me make a home where poetry can happen, and to CAConrad for always making sure my poems make it into this world.